PROVENCE

Photographs by
Sonja Bullaty
& Angelo Lomeo

Text by
Marie-Ange Guillaume

Abbeville Press Publishers
New York London Paris

jacket, front and
pages 18-19
*fields of lavender and
sunflowers
Mont Ventoux region*

jacket, back and
page 37
*reflections
Martigues*

page 1
*sunflowers
Bonnieux*

pages 2-3
*fields of lavender
Mont Ventoux region*

page 4
*grove of fruit trees
Les Alpilles*

page 5
*poplars behind a stone wall
Gordes*

pages 6-7
*Saint-Paul-de-Mausole,
monastery / convalescent home,
where van Gogh lived
Saint-Rémy-de-Provence*

page 9: top
*detail on Roman sarcophagus
at the Alyscamps
Arles*

page 9: bottom
*flower pot
Saint-Rémy-de-Provence*

pages 10-11
*Van Gogh Square
Arles*

EDITOR: Susan Costello
DESIGNER: Patricia Fabricant
TRANSLATOR: John Goodman
PRODUCTION EDITOR: Alice Gray
COPYEDITOR: Clifford Browder
PRODUCTION SUPERVISOR: Matthew Pimm
MAP: Claudia Carlson

First Edition

10 9 8 7 6 5

Library of Congress Cataloging-in-Publication Data

Bullaty, Sonja.
        Provence / photographs by Sonja Bullaty and Angelo Lomeo; text by
Marie-Ange Guillaume.
        p. cm.
ISBN 1-55859-557-0

1. Provence (France)—Pictorial works. 2. Provence (France) in art. 3. Provence
(France) in literature. I. Lomeo, Angelo. II. Guillaume, M.A. (Marie-Ange) III.
Title.
DC611.P958B85 1993   93-9885
944'.9—dc20   CIP

N

Villefranche

NICE

Saint-Paul-de-Vence

Gourdon

CANNES

ALPES-DE-HAUTE-PROVENCE

Sisteron

VAUCLUSE

PLATEAU

Valensole

Riez

MONT VENTOUX

Sault

Vaison-la-Romaine

LES DENTELLES
DE MONTMIRAIL

Le Barroux

Roussillon

LUBÉRON REGION

Jouques

ORANGE

Bonnieux

Gordes

Lourmarin

SAINTE-VICTOIRE
MOUNTAIN

Ardèche River

Ménerbes

Vauvenargues

Cross of Provence

AVIGNON

Durance River

Villeneuve-les-Avignon

Chateaurenard

AIX-EN-PROVENCE

TOULON

Saint-Rémy-
de-Provence

Eygalières

Uzès

LES ANTIQUES

PROVENCE

Tarascon

Les Baux-de-Provence

MARSEILLES

Cassis

LES ALPILLES

NÎMES

ARLES

Martigues

CAMARGUE

Rhône River

MEDITERRANEAN SEA

Saintes-Maries-de-la-Mer

Kilometers

0   10   20   30

0   5   10   15

Miles

CONTENTS

In Search of
Light and Paradise
10

Fields
42

Lavender and
Sunflowers
60

Farm Life
80

Windows
88

Villages
106

Stonework
128

Cities
148

Landscapes and
Seascapes
162

Index
179

IN SEARCH OF LIGHT AND PARADISE

*Cézanne's studio
Aix-en-Provence*

The House in the Vineyard

It's six o'clock in the evening and the village is still flooded with sunlight. You buy some Provence rosé at a local shop that also sells children's swimming pools, artificial flowers, real peaches, chaises longues, screwdrivers, vegetables, and even a *single* dress—just in case. You stroke the cat stretched out on a blue chair near a blue window, or perhaps on the hot stone rim of the fountain, and wind your way back up the hill. On the opposite slope a golden haze envelops the vineyards, obscuring them from view.

The house is at the end of a dusty road, lost in the song of the cicadas—who don't sing at all, of course, not even in "ancient Greek" as van Gogh thought: they click. Deep in the Midi one can no longer tell whether it's their clamor that dazzles or the light. Now they go to it with a will, as if trying to slow the fall of night. They're making up for lost time, they're holding fast to their short lives. Three years of larval, subterranean existence for a few weeks of light. All we know of the cicada, this invisible uproar, is the noise of its nuptials. These begin in late June, and toward the end of August the exhausted insect lays its eggs, drops to the foot of its tree, and dies, devoured by neighboring ants. La Fontaine was prone to euphemism: "mating done, utterly stunned"; in reality, the poor thing was totally digested.

The house at the end of the road is drowning in oleanders, geraniums, and mimosas. One could spend hours at a time seated on the warm stone of its little wall, watching the summer vibrate above the vineyards. Beyond the shed with its three cypresses, there's nothing but transparent sky and ocher earth, torpid after the hot day. Everything in this world is so beautiful, everything is so pure, including the mountains behind which the sun is about to disappear, that you envision returning here one day to remain for a thousand years.

"Naturally you love Provence. But which Provence?"—Colette

There's more here than the sweetness of things and the exuberance of flowers. There's also rocky, solitary terrain eroded by winter, ice, and hurricanes. And there's Le Ventoux, very well named (*vent,* "wind"), on whose slopes a small poppy from Greenland flourishes. At the beginning of the century, after publication of the first *Tourist Guide to Mount Ventoux,* women dressed in bear skins could be seen climbing it to applaud the magic of the rising sun. But most of the time it's the domain of sheep that turn over its rocks in search of a bit of soft grass.

There are fountains and Roman ghosts, fields of lavender and oceans of sunflowers. Marvelous villages invaded by Martians in shorts, barbecues in the open sun, art galleries that double as *crêperies*. There are cities and crowds drawn by festivals. Petrarch, who loved Provence, detested Avignon, speaking of it from the depths of his fourteenth century in terms not so different from those of a festival-goer today who finds the hubbub of its crowds eminently resistible: "It's a sewer in which all the filth of the universe ends up. There God is scorned. There money is worshiped, human and divine laws are trodden underfoot. Everything about it reeks of deceit—the air, the earth, the houses, and above all the bedrooms."

And then there's the sea. "I am a child of the mountains, I hate the sea, it terrifies me," wrote Giono. Pagnol, who was born in Aubagne and rarely traveled farther north, was unfamiliar with northern Provence. What common thread ties together its dry plateaus, the Mediterranean, and the lights of its old port; the fields of sunflowers and the lugubrious silhouette of Sade's château; Colette, who professed to crush garlic "as if committing murder," and van Gogh, who cut off his ear to soothe his pain? There are a thousand and one Provences, and their sole shared trait is excess—of colors, climates, passion—and ravishment.

To be sure, a popular dictum has it that olive trees refuse to grow above Nyons. As the olive is an indisputable "proof" of Provence, one might say that its northern limit is Nyons. To the west, though kept in check by the Rhône, it nonetheless overflows into the Camargue—that other planet that the ancients took to be the antechamber to the Land of Shades—and it was at Saintes-Maries-de-la-Mer that van Gogh, seeing the Mediterranean for the first time, found it to be "the color of mackerel." To the east, Provence extends as far as Antibes, where Nicolas de Staël went to paint and die above the ramparts. But outside of these subjective geographic markers, each of us finds the Provence of his or her dreams—rooted in the striking realities of the real one.

"In this parceled-out land, purchased by the square meter, rented out by the week, open day and night, I'm most attached to what remains strangely harsh and imperturbable." —*Colette*

Deeply enamored of the veiled sunlight of the Channel, Colette was fifty-three when she fell in love with the south of France and bought a house in Saint-Tropez. "I found it by the side of a road that scares off automobiles," she wrote, apparently annoyed— already in 1926—by the ubiquity of tourists. "They drive, stop to drink, sweat, then drive on and drink again. They say: 'This region would be delightful if only it weren't so hot and the food were bearable.' Everywhere they clamor for their steak and potatoes, cooked just right, their eggs and bacon, their fresh spinach and favorite coffee."

At the Treille Muscate, as this house was known, where Paul Géraldy, Dunoyer de Segonzac, and Francis Carco came to lunch on the terrace beneath the shade of a wisteria, there were orgies of garlic mayonnaise, bouillabaisse, allspice, and olive oil. Life was lived, at least for a time, with the pleasure and intensity of first love. Colette described her existence at the Treille Muscate in 1926 and, rereading the text four years later, was herself amazed: "It's very touching, this lyricism of first encounters. . . . I write of mussing the vines. Mussing the vines! What can have been running through my head? Vines, when they're green, one ties them down, and when they're dried out, one cuts them—very short, if you please." She also dreamed of having a Provençal garden that was wild, unkempt. But in fact her gardener—"a charming dark man with frizzy body hair"—favored impeccable rectangles and scrupulous geometries. She rebelled, for the result looked like a "barbecue grill." And the frizzy man answered her very patiently, in a thick Provençal accent tinged with regret: "Ah! If only I could do otherwise. If only it were easy to shift things around. Already last year you had me plant reeds facing the other way, and by August nothing was left of them." He explained to her that the sun dictated that particular placement. Perfection is not of this world, however, and in the end she got her garden of "raging flowers" thanks to God, the mistral, deep frosts, and hardy survivors. But she ended up asking herself what there was about it that was particularly Provençal in character. Nothing: no ornamental vegetables, none of the typical disorder. No rare flowers, "but a privileged sky extends above it," and this was the secret. "Now I know what a Provençal garden is: it's a garden whose superiority over all others derives from one thing only—from its flowering in Provence."

"In short, I think life here is a happier thing than in countless other spots on the earth."—Vincent van Gogh

Van Gogh arrived in Arles in February 1888. He came "to see another light," a clearer sky. He wrote his brother Theo letters full of ardor and enthusiasm. He came in search of Japan and found it in "the limpidity of the air and the gay color effects." On other occasions he preferred to see it as Holland, or even as "the Africa close to oneself." He rented a little yellow house with green shutters in the Place Lamartine and sent Theo a sketch of it "under a sulphur sun, under a pure cobalt sky." For the sake of clarity he wrote "blue" in the middle of his drawing's black and white sky.

His first spring there he was seized by a furious desire to work, for he wanted "to do a Provence orchard that has a monstrous gaiety." Beside another sketch in which the grass is "very very green" and the sky "very very blue," he expressed concern about the neurological health of all these extravagant flowers: "These blessed plants flourish to such an extent that some might well become afflicted with locomotor ataxia." On the other hand, this floral energy was contrasted with a human lassitude that troubled him. "These aren't the hearty laborers of the North. They seem to work slackly, left-handedly, without enthusiasm." He saw this mode of living in the sun, this systematic refusal of unnecessary exertion, as "the ruin of the Midi."

Signac, who settled in Saint-Tropez in 1892, painted in small strokes of blue, green, and pink but saw "nothing but white" in the local landscape. For him, while the North was *colored,* the Midi was *luminous.* When van Gogh ordered paints from Theo, they were an orgy of Veronese green, zinc white, chrome yellow, ultramarine, geranium lacquer, Prussian blue, cobalt, and vermilion. And then he hesitated, not wanting to ruin his brother, telling him he could economize on the blues for the skies. "If you're strapped, I can make do perfectly well without the expensive blues and the carmine. One tube of Prussian blue takes the place of six ultramarines or cobalts and costs a third as much."

The summer arrived, with its "quite glorious intense heat." Vincent saw it as the triumph of yellow, of all possible yellows. (Nicolas de Staël would see the Mediterranean as red.) He worked right through the day, in full sunlight, happy "as a cicada." He painted the haystacks and the market gardens of La Crau, an oasis reclaimed from a forbidding, mysterious desert of stones. Aristotle suggested that all these rocks had risen to the surface in an earthquake. According to Aeschylus, Zeus was responsible, having rained them down from the heavens to assist Hercules in his battle with the Ligurians. They're still there. Not far away, even more sinister, the road over the crest of the Alpilles—van Gogh insisted on calling them the Alpines—crosses the so-called Valley of Hell, whose cataclysmic geography and collapsing rock formations are reputed to have so impressed Dante, passing through on his way to Les Baux, that they influenced the description of the nine circles of his *Inferno.* The village of Les Baux, perched on a rock, its buildings merging into the cliffs with disquieting ease, participates in this chaos. The citadel, the ancient abode of the counts of Baux, has been a gutted ruin ever since Louis XIII ordered it destroyed. When Alexandre Dumas came to the village, it was dead. All the doors and windows were open but no one was living in its houses. The only life he encountered there was also imbued with death: in the church the body of a young girl lay in a coffin, and a dozen beggars were taking part in a funeral ceremony without a priest. In van Gogh's time the town was still abandoned, battered on all sides by the winds. Today it reassumes its ghostly beauty in winter, but in the summer it has the air of an Arab bazaar, with overpriced restaurants and souvenir shops. Selling souvenirs of what? Of the time when the counts of Baux, proud of their presumed Visigothic ancestry, threw their prisoners from its towers?

"Unfortunately, in addition to the sun of the good Lord, three-fourths of the time there's the Devil's mistral."—van Gogh

It was at Saintes-Maries-de-la-Mer that van Gogh's first view of the Mediterranean reduced him to total redundancy: he vowed to "still intensify the color even more." He became obsessed, thought the future of art was in the Midi, dreamed of creating a studio where other painters would come to work in an amiable, relaxed atmosphere, and invited Gauguin to be the first of these painter friends.

While waiting he continued to work. He pitched his easel even when the mistral blew, waging combat with it. Later he would ask with touching naivete whether the awkwardness of some of Cézanne's studies might not result from their having been executed in the mistral. "His easel was shaking," he wrote, as if he'd solved an enigma.

The mistral already had a bad reputation, and it was perhaps superfluous to see it as the cause of Cézanne's "awkwardnesses." It prompted the ringing of alarm bells, carried off sheep like balls of cotton, and sowed discord in households to such an extent that—in earlier times—it was considered an attenuating circumstance if a man killed his wife while it was blowing. What was the source of this mysterious wind? An ancient legend tells of a village in the Vivarais, surrounded by marshlands and dominated by a pierced rock: the mistral emerged from this rock until one day the inhabitants resolved to stop the hole with a door, which they opened from time to time to clear away the miasmas of the marsh. A century ago the inhabitants of Morières, close to Avignon, sent a delegation to ask if they might consider opening the door a bit less frequently. Legends can be tenacious.

As for Madame de Sévigné, who sojourned at Grignan three times and subsequently died there, she sent horrified letters to her friends about the snow, the ice, her numb fingers and frozen inkwells, the fury of the Rhône ("Do you still think the Rhône is just water?" she asked Madame de Grignan, who had barely escaped being borne away by it), and of course the mistral, which she suspected of being none other than "the Devil" himself.

17

In any case, it seems that since the request from the people of Morières, the mistral has calmed somewhat. But van Gogh continued to feel that studies he'd executed in its winds had the same "wild air" as those of Cézanne's.

He painted the old peasant Patience Escalier, a starry night, and the Alcazar café, trying "to express the power of darkness in a low-life tavern. Beneath an appearance of Japanese gaiety and a simplicity like that of *Tartarin*." van Gogh loved Daudet's novel of that name. Later, after Gauguin's departure, he was overwhelmed by sadness at the thought that his guest might not even have read *Tartarin sur les Alpes*. But for the time being he rose every day at dawn to capture the ephemeral splendor of sunflowers. "With the heartiness of a Marseillais eating bouillabaisse," he worked on three paintings of these radiant blooms, these mad stars, and imagined producing a dozen or so to hang in the studio where he awaited Gauguin "with intense emotion."

"You see that my luck in the Midi is no better than in the North. Everywhere it's pretty much the same."—van Gogh

Gauguin moved into the yellow house on October 20, 1888. He didn't like Arles, finding it "small and shabby, the landscape and the people." He didn't share his host's enthusiasm for sunflowers. "They're just flowers," he said. Vincent wrote to Theo at great length about how much he thought of Gauguin, but the atmosphere soured quickly and they soon began to argue about everything—from Delacroix and Monticelli to the inedible soup concocted by Vincent. Gauguin began to speak of his departure. On December 24 he showed Vincent the portrait he'd made of him painting sunflowers. Vincent recognized himself in it, but a self "gone mad." That evening at the café he threw a glass at Gauguin, who then genuinely resolved to leave. The story of the severed ear that ensued is well known. Vincent's name first appeared in print in an account of this incident in the *Forum républicain,* an Arles newspaper: "Sunday night, at eleven-thirty in the evening, one Vincent van Gogh, an artist of Dutch origin, presented himself at licensed brothel no. 1, asked for one Rachel, and presented her with his ear, saying to her: 'Guard this object carefully.' Then he disappeared."

Gauguin left and van Gogh entered a hospital. All had not been lost, however. Together they had painted the Alyscamps burial ground, producing very different images— one serenely geometric, the other more tormented—despite the use of flamboyant autumnal colors common to both. And then van Gogh would execute a painting of a woman of Arles based on a drawing by Gauguin, to whom he wrote (using a theoretical term dear to

fields of lavender and
sunflowers
Mont Ventoux region

Gauguin): "It is, if you will, a synthesis of an *Arlésienne;* as syntheses of *Arlésiennes* are rare, think of it as a work by you and me, as a summary of our months of work together."

After several hospital stays and bouts of madness, the "poor yellow house" was closed up, and in May 1889 van Gogh entered the asylum in Saint-Rémy-de-Provence. In the year spent at "the menagerie" he executed a hundred drawings and a hundred and fifty paintings. At this time he found himself particularly drawn to cypresses, which he considered to be "the opposite and yet the equivalent" of sunflowers, being especially partial to their shade of green, which he saw as having "a distinguished quality." He hastened to paint as much as possible between crises, but he was somewhat unnerved by the allure these trees were taking on, full as they were of "jumbled, atrocious religious ideas" that had never occurred to him in the North. He was increasingly obsessed by a desire to return there, as if the vivid colors of the South were a source of pain, whereas the North might cure him. In February he painted for Theo's newborn child a flowering almond branch against a saturated blue sky. The almond tree, provider of the season's first blossoms, sometimes even under the snow—the glory of springtime, the embodiment of natural renewal at its most fervent. This canvas "was perhaps the most patiently worked and the best thing I had done, painted with calm and a greater firmness of touch. And the next day, down like a brute." A new crisis had felled him, during which, indifferent to the Provençal spring, he painted his *Memories of the North.*

He had resolved to leave, though the prospect filled him with "great regret." Seeing the Provençal landscape refreshed by the rain one last time, he expressed sorrow over all the canvases he hadn't yet painted there, but all the same he left.

"Look, your papa is talking to himself in the garden."
"No, he's not talking to himself, he's talking to the olive tree."
—Little girls in conversation

The little girl's father was Jacques Prévert, and he was in his garden in Saint-Paul-de-Vence. If he was talking to the olive tree, perhaps this was because in a sense it had "done him a favor." For Prévert's Provence—first in wartime, then in time of peace—was made after its image: vibrant and generous, peopled with a crowd of friends, the site of incessant work, whether films, books, or dreams.

In 1940 Prévert refused to fight in the war—he detested slaughter of all kinds, whether legal or not. A Protestant, he went to live in Tourrettes-sur-Loup, in a house clinging to a vertiginous slope of the Loup River gorge, where—a rare luxury in this hallucinatory environment—he took his baths in a hollow of the rock itself. With the aid of Vincent, a young innkeeper who also hated slaughter and who got drunk with his pigs before killing them, Prévert hid his Jewish friends threatened by Nazi barbarity: among them, the production designer Alexandre Trauner and the musician Joseph Kosma, clandestine participants in Prévert's cinematic endeavors whose names would appear in the credits only after the war.

Les Visiteurs du soir (The Evening Visitors) was shot in La Garoupe, near Antibes, which created all sorts of problems. The extras, for instance, were so hungry that when unleashed on a piece of beef figuring in a banquet scene, they devoured it so quickly that Carné didn't have time to get all the shots he'd wanted. A year later, reunited in a house close to Vence, this team put together the project for Les Enfants du paradis (Children of Paradise). None of them yet suspected that this film would be a monument of French cinema, but they all put their hearts into it. Kosma composed the score as quickly as Prévert could write the script. Trauner designed the sets and Mayo the costumes, while the future stars, Arletty, Pierre Brasseur, and Jean-Louis Barrault, paid them periodic visits.

> "My name is Garance."
> "Garance—that's pretty."
> "It's the name of a flower."
> "One that's red, like your lips."
> —Prévert, Les Enfants du paradis

Not at all. Though Arletty is an unforgettable flower of liberty in the film, the garance is not a red flower. It is a plant imported from Smyrna in the eighteenth century and long cultivated in the Vaucluse for the dyes produced from its roots: for quite some time soldiers were sent off to war rigged out in pantalons garance (bright red pants), until it was realized that this brilliant color was ill suited to camouflage. But Prévert was a poet, and in Arletty's mouth the garance will always remain a red flower.

An enormous set of the Boulevard du Crime was built in the Victorine studios in Nice. Shooting began in August 1943—with, for some scenes, as many as 1,800 extras—and was interrupted several times, notably because of an announced Allied landing that never took place and wartime damage done to the sets. The film was finally released in March 1945.

The war over, Prévert returned to his Parisian life. It was a stupid accident that sent him back to the Midi. In October 1948, after participating in a French radio broadcast, he mistakenly walked through a picture window on the building's second floor and plunged to the sidewalk of the Champs-Elysées. After an extended coma he left to convalesce in Saint-Paul-de-Vence with his wife, his young daughter, and as always, a whole crowd of nomad friends. Yves Montand and Simone Signoret came to celebrate their marriage, to which he was a witness. Chagall lived close by in Vence, and Braque, Picasso, and Miró were frequent visitors. Marcel Duhamel, director of the Série Noir (which Prévert himself had baptized), lived on the ramparts of Antibes. This joyous social bustle did not make for a relaxing convalescence, though it lasted for several years.

While his song "Les Feuilles mortes," recorded in the United States as "Autumn Leaves," was becoming popular throughout the world, Prévert returned to Paris in 1955 and settled in Montmartre, but he continued to spend his summers in Antibes. It was there that Audiberti, following the ancient example set by Demosthenes, strode up and down the beach reciting poetry with his mouth full of pebbles. Nor has Antibes forgotten the legendary silhouette of Prévert, who from daybreak walked his dog around its port, chatted with the fish sellers, the street violinist Giordano, and the cheese seller, whom he encouraged to become a poet so energetically that he followed this advice. He took Chagall and Marcel Mouloudji to visit his favorite antique dealer and joyously traversed the entire Riviera with his great friend Picasso. Together they produced a book entitled *Diurnes (Day Pieces),* "because people are sick of nocturnes," said Prévert. Then he exhibited his collages in the Château Grimaldi in Antibes, where paintings by Picasso were being shown on the main floor. In 1968, sympathetic to the students participating in the May uprisings, he published *Arbres,* which was infused with his love for certain "creatures" that he saw pounded by the fierce sun every year. "All alone, an olive tree desperately throws upward toward a calcinated sky its two singed arms like a lynched negro."

"The limber fire leaped over the heather as the bell sounded three a.m."
—Jean Giono

So begins the terrible conflagration in *Colline (Hill of Destiny)* that was to unite the inhabitants of Bastides Blanches, "a wreck of a hamlet" lost between the plain and the mountains of Lure.

Giono was born in Manosque in 1885 and died there in 1970. He was a creature of the mountains, a man of wild landscapes, windy villages, and century-old oaks. He wasn't crazy for the sun. What he loved was the darker, more violent aspect of Provence, and day's end. "Then—if we're wise—we'll walk sedately toward the fountains in the profound darkness of the night." The area over which he roamed began at

Durance and ended at Ventoux. Not out of provincialism—least of all, in that for him this landscape was interior. "There is no Provence. Whoever loves it loves the world or loves nothing." Had it been up to him, he'd have preferred to live in Scotland in the rain. But this was his birthplace, and he sought in its hills what he would have sought anywhere else: a universe in harmony with man, sensuality, and the "fullness of days." Still, there is reason to think that the terrible beauty of Provence suited his dream perfectly, that he would not have found this particular brand of ecstatic sensuality in Scotland: "We are the world. I was completely spread out, my belly and palms flat against the earth. The sky weighed down on my back, touched the birds who touched the trees."

Needless to say that such transport, such exaltation was totally ill suited to a coast along which "azure was marketed like tuna." He was repelled by this "open-air sexual marketplace" (*foutoir en plein air*), this whorish land that yields without flinching to "the flood of Parisians, Belgians, English, and Eskimos" en route to the Mediterranean. Here again, it wasn't a question of moral scruples or virtue—his books are full of defrocked priests, thieves, whores, and deserters—but of a personal aesthetic. He loved "the real country," proud and secretive, the one not up for sale.

Visitors to the Château d'If are shown the "authentic" dungeons of the Count of Monte Christo and the abbé Faria, both of them imaginary prisoners. As for Giono, he was actually incarcerated in 1939 in Fort Saint-Nicolas on Marseilles's old port for having refused, like Prévert, to fight in the war. Curiously, he wrote of having spent some of the happiest hours of his life there, and made Marseilles into a kind of visionary city: "For the people of Manosque, Marseilles was a kind of Moscow. . . . Every evening, as soon as the lights went out, underneath each bed a kind of fog materialized within which appeared a golden city. . . . It was Marseilles." He became a kind of "sailor" after cotranslating *Moby Dick,* adding Melville's white whale to his personal obsessions. The mountain was an abyss, and so was the sea. For Giono it would never be that blue amenity bordered "by miles of naked women drying themselves out." And Marseilles would never be a matter of *pétanque* (a variant of the game known as *boules*), bouillabaisse, and other elements of local color easily digested by tourists.

"And shellfish, my friend, and bouillabaisses, the food of a thundering God breathing fire into my body."—Letter from Emile Zola to Gustave Flaubert

They all came to Marseilles, they all had their moment describing this dazzling melting pot of colors, races, and odors, this old port where all the mullets and scorpion fish of the Mediterranean, lifted from blue boats, come to die in crates. Chateaubriand was reminded of Constantinople, while Flaubert saw it as a kind of Alexandria, "a Capernaum, a Babel of all nations." George Sand saw in the port the same dirty water figuring in her *Mare au diable (The Devil's Pool)*, but in the end she succumbed to the charm of the locals: "We're making do, however, because at heart its inhabitants are good." Chopin, in that plural voice that is the prerogative of lovers, wrote: "Marseilles is ugly, it's an old but not an ancient city, it bores us." Lamartine found it "a country of generosity, heart, and genuine poetry." Going against her prevailing view, Madame de Sévigné declared herself to be "ravished by this city's singular beauty,' but reverted to her habitual dour assessment when the elements became capricious: "The weather's taken a dastardly turn. We can see neither sea nor ship nor stronghold." Later in Paris, she recalled with emotion "the pretty whirlwind of Marseilles."

This whirlwind is given concentrated expression in the poster that Albert Dubout made for *Fanny,* the film by Marcel Pagnol (and Marc Allégret). The full gamut of Marseilles folklore is included at the port: *pétanque* players and their supporters, fish sellers, advertisements for Pastis and the Magali store chain—all jumbled together in an inextricable agglomeration of jolly good fellows: an image of universal merrymaking, jovial and motley, terrifically noisy for a poster. Bearing in mind that Pagnol and Giono, at the peak of their careers, "almost" worked together, we're not surprised to learn that their relations were affectionate and stormy by turns. In 1933 Pagnol made a short movie, *Jofroy*, based on a story by Giono, who felt he'd been "annexed, devoured, and transformed," then allowed himself more positive feelings: after all, the two peasants who had inspired the tale recognized perfect likenesses of themselves on the screen! In 1934 Pagnol based his film *Angèle* on Giono's novel *Un de Beaumugnes (One from Beaumugnes)*. Once again the writer was somewhat ambivalent about seeing himself "pagnolisé." In 1937 Pagnol made *Regain (Harvest)*, based on *Jean le Bleu (Blue Boy)*, and Giono, reconciled, became fascinated by the mad enterprise of reconstructing his ruined village of Aubignane in Barres-de-Saint-Esprit: "It was a question of building ruins. As soon as a wall rose beneath the masons' hands, it aged under those same hands and in their heads." But he found the final result "breathless, bombastic, and excessive." When Pagnol followed this pattern again in *La Femme du boulanger (The Baker's Wife),* another film adapted from *Jean le Bleu* and hailed as a masterpiece, Giono took him to court. Each reproached the other for having violated their contract, and each was found guilty—and won a half victory. Pagnol never again made a film based on Giono's work. And yet . . .

"Then the spell was cast and I felt a love begin that was to last the rest of my life."—Marcel Pagnol

Pagnol was not only Marius, Fanny, Raimu, César, Panisse, Escartefigue, and "You're breaking my heart." He had every reason to love the peasants and the hills in Giono, for he, too, was from the mountains: he was born in Aubagne, "beneath the Garlaban crowned with goats," in the rocks and brush, only a few miles from Canebière, despite its radically different topography. His family had lived in Provence for centuries and his grandfather, who resided in Valréas and then Marseilles, was a stonecutter—an artist who, in his rare free time, brought his family and friends to the foot of the Pont du Gard for picnics. While the others amused themselves in more conventional ways, he strode over the aqueduct examining its joints and caressing its stone. Then, seated in the grass, he would contemplate it until evening. "This is why, thirty years later, his sons and daughters, at the mere mention of the Pont du Gard, lifted their eyes toward the heavens and breathed long sighs."

From Aubagne he went to Saint-Loup, a village in the suburbs of Marseilles, then to Marseilles itself. But Madame Pagnol needed pure air and one day Joseph Pagnol—the father—announced the good news: they were to spend their summer vacation at a villa in the hills, "on the edge of the Garrigue desert." This was in April; vacation didn't start until July, and young Marcel, who was nine, tirelessly repeated the magic words: villa, pine forests, cicadas . . . He'd already seen a few cicadas, but his father was promising him thousands!

The great day finally arrived. While the furniture was being moved by wagon, the family departed for the promised land, first by streetcar and then on foot, marching for hours beneath a beating sun, clambering, scampering, and scaling to the point of exhaustion—an outing that was "a bit long" but "hygienic," according to the father. It was there, after the last village and the final faint pathways were behind them, and he was confronted by the immensity of pine forests coming "to die like waves at the foot of three rocky summits," that young Marcel discovered his world of liberty, magic, and tenderness. And it was there that he returned to construct his ruined Aubignane for *Regain*. And it was perhaps as an homage to that late July—during which, in the summer torpor and as a preparation for his vacation, the schoolmaster had read him Alphonse Daudet—that in 1954 he made Daudet's *Lettres de mon moulin* (*Letters from My Mill*) his last film.

"A ruin, this mill; a crumbling debris of stone, iron, and old planks that hadn't been turned by the wind for years and was utterly prostrate, its members broken, as useless as a poet."—Alphonse Daudet

The mill cracking under pressure from the north wind stimulated in Daudet memories of the sea, of lighthouses and distant islands. Finding that it satisfied his "taste for isolation and savagery," he spent entire days there with his old dog Miracle, a spaniel who'd been saved from a wrecked ship by fishermen. He even wanted to buy this mill and consulted with the notary of Fontvieille about its purchase, but this project never came to fruition. Perhaps because the day he brought his wife there, "the north wind, seeing this Parisian woman hostile to sun and wind, amused itself by tumbling her about and knocking her down." Maybe the new Madame Daudet didn't much like being tumbled about and knocked down. However that may be, the pretty, spotless mill—hardly a "ruin"—that today is made out to be Daudet's never had anything to do with him. But it was indeed there that he came every winter "to heal himself of Paris and its restlessness," even if he went back to Paris to actually write his *Lettres.* He hunted in the Camargue and rejoined his poet friends in the Alyscamps "among the gray stone sarcophagi," or in the village of Les Baux, then no more than "a dusty pile of ruins." And also on the island of Barthelasse, opposite the ramparts of Avignon. There everyone drank wine from the papal vineyards and danced, but not on the bridge, because it had been broken long since.

Have you ever heard the "true" story of the Avignon bridge? It was built by an eleven-year-old child! In 1177—the day of a solar eclipse, it would seem—the divine voice addressed a young shepherd named Bénezet and asked him to construct a bridge over the Rhône. The child protested: he knew nothing about bridges or rivers, and this river was particularly treacherous. But the voice was insistent and the child went to see the bishop, who made fun of him and sent him to the town provost, who also made fun of him. For if no architect had ever succeeded in doing this, how could he? From this point on, versions of the story differ somewhat, but in every case they illustrate how faith can move mountains, recounting how young Bénezet effortlessly lifted an enormous stone normally impossible to budge—even with thirty men—and placed it at the river's edge, at the point from which the first arch would spring. The assembled crowd was smitten with admiration and the provost gave three hundred sous to Bénezet for the purchase of other stones and labor. It is said that the bridge was completed in 1185, and also that Bénezet died in 1184 at age nineteen. In any case, the bridge was severed in 1226, rebuilt in 1237, and definitively broken by the furious battering of an ice floe during the winter of 1670.

Daudet's windmill near Arles

27

After what he called his "lyric escapades," Daudet returned to the silence of his mill and dreamed of the book he would later fill with its songs and laughter, with the sun and the smells of the hills. *Lettres de mon Moulin* would remain his favorite book, not from a literary point of view, but because it always reminded him of the sweetest hours of his youth. And ever since, the mill "turns in the sun, a poet restored to the wind, a dreamer brought back to life," forever.

"If you ever come to Provence, our farmers will often speak to you of 'la cabro de moussu Seguin, que se battegue touto la nevi emé lou loup, e piei lou matin lou loup la mangé.'"—Alphonse Daudet

Translation: "M. Seguin's goat, which fought all night with a wolf, and then in the morning the wolf ate it." As a child, I hated the very idea of Provence—all that thyme and wild herbs, all those windmills—because of this horrible ending that ruined my life. Admittedly I should have been prepared, for the story begins badly, with M. Seguin already having lost six goats. Each one had grown tired of its enclosure, broken its cord, and made for the mountains where it was eaten by a wolf. But the seventh, Blanquette, was such a lovely little goat that one dared hope the best for her. She escapes, too, of course, and then Daudet paints a picture of the mountains that is pure joy: tender grass, perfume, golden broom, clear streams, warm sunlight, freedom, love—all seen through the eyes of a young goat. Gamboling everywhere, Blanquette's joy increased: "One would have said that ten of M. Seguin's goats were on the mountain." But night falls, the little creature becomes disoriented, and our hopes dim. She watches M. Seguin's house disappear in the haze, she hears the clanging bells of a returning flock, and for the first time she thinks of the wolf. As expected, the wolf comes and eats her, and I've never been able to accept this ending—the very antithesis of fairy-tale endings—nor her "beautiful white fur all stained with blood," nor Daudet's sadistic snuffing out of this longing for freedom.

"What condition is it in, this château? And my poor park, does one still recognize something of me in it?" —Donatien Alphonse François de Sade, Marquis de Sade

Everything is relative, and if "sadism" exists, memories of it should be sought in the ruins of the Château de Lacoste. Donatien de Sade was twenty-three when he arrived for the first time in this village at the foot of the Luberon. He was thirty-seven when he was incarcerated at Vincennes. In the interim, in the course of his many visits to London (or La Coste, as it was then known), it seems that he modernized the château and gave far too many fêtes, then entrenched himself there without renouncing his insatiable libertinism. Sade was not a vicious murderer like Gilles de Rais, nor the "horrible, ignominious monster" described by the *Revue aptésienne* in 1835, nor even the "appalling madman" of Michelet. According to the villagers, he was nothing more than "un fameux pistachie"—a confounded lecher. (But then, some of this local indulgence must be attributed to the fact that Sade was savvy enough to obtain his girls and boys far from the village.) At the time theater was all the rage, and every château had to have its own stage. Sade built a theater that was a hundred meters square, recruited several successive troupes, gave balls and suppers, and accumulated considerable debt. To be sure, the theatricals in question did not remain on an exclusively literary plane; because he involved servants (and others) of both sexes in forbidden acts—sodomy was punishable by death—in the end, Sade drew the wrath of justice. He was not the only debauchee of the period—far from it—but rumor deformed and exaggerated his exploits to the point of making him out to be a murderer—erroneously and absurdly, since no reported deaths were involved. He was arrested and escaped. Arrested again, he escaped once more and sought refuge one last time in La Coste. He was taken yet again, and this time remained incarcerated in the prison of Vincennes, returning to La Coste only twenty years later. The château, which was first pillaged and then sold, abandoned, and thrashed by the mistral and the rain, slowly became the ruin that still dominates the charming village and the Café de Sade.

(Thanks to its present owner, who is restoring it rather fastidiously and has protected the site by purchasing the surrounding land, it has been safeguarded from promotional exploitation.) So it still stands, a morass of brambles and collapsing stone walls, half living and half dead in the night of time. André Breton made a pilgrimage there, but it sometimes happens that ill-informed tourists, thinking Sade a contemporary, inquire nervously whether he ever comes to check on the construction work!

Not so far off, houses, terrain, and cliffs blend together in a blood-colored phantasmagoria. The ocher quarries of Roussillon, sculpted by wind and rain, seem to bathe in endless sunset, even in shadow, even by night. In reality, if this landscape seems imbued with every conceivable nuance of ocher, red, and gold, that's because it remembers the blood of Sirmonde: Raymond and Sirmonde of Avignon lived here, and Raymond, who spent the day hunting, asked his page to keep his wife company while he was away. Predictably enough, while fulfilling this charge the page fell deeply in love

clouds
Mont Ventoux

with her. Mad with rage, Raymond killed the page and, during a banquet, ordered Sirmonde to eat his heart. The poor woman threw herself off a cliff and was crushed on the rocks below. Legend has it that the earth of the region acquired its color of eternal twilight from her blood.

"A certain harmony of colors unrelated to reality expresses the relation of his most intimate self to the universe."—Georges Braque

In 1870 Cézanne, fleeing the draft at the time of the Franco-Prussian War, sought refuge in L'Estaque, among the bare rocks and wild terrain in which his friend Emile Zola had spent his youth. Zola always cherished his memories of this landscape: "The red earth bleeds, the pines sparkle like emeralds, the brilliant white of freshly washed laundry stands out against the rocks." It was here that Cézanne, discovering the "frightening" sun on the red roofs, the hills, and the sea, wrote to Pissarro: "It seems to me that objects stand out in silhouette not only in black and white, but in blue, red, brown, and violet. I could be mistaken, but this strikes me as the opposite of conventional modeling." An important discovery, not only for Cézanne—who would attempt to render the effect created by the perpetual movement of this light over objects solely by means of color rhythms—but for all the painters who followed in the footsteps of the "master from Aix."

Born in Aix-en-Provence, where he befriended Zola in school, Cézanne abandoned his law studies to go to Paris; but, proud of his Provençal origins, he obstinately retained his southern accent and always returned to "this old native ground that's so vibrant, so rugged," to paint precariously perched towns, the twisted trunks of olive trees, and of course Mont Sainte-Victoire, whose secret geometry he was determined to transfigure. What he sought—and his quest would be rife with implications for the history of painting—was a "harmony parallel to that of nature," one that, in its focus on individual sensation, was more profoundly faithful to nature than any kind of realism.

In 1882 Renoir, who had known Cézanne in Paris and maintained almost fraternal relations with him, visited him in L'Estaque. Some years later they painted together in the environs of Aix. Then Renoir settled definitively in Cagnes-sur-Mer, in a modest house at the foot of the hill that on one side overlooked the old town—a labyrinth of courtyards and narrow streets pressed against the steep terrain—and on the other side, between palm trees and oleanders, the sea. (La Marina did not yet spoil the view of the horizon.) "In this marvelous landscape, it's as though misfortune can't reach you," he said. Before long he would have to fix his brush to his fingers, which were deformed by illness, and have himself carried where he wanted to go, but he continued to paint, with a formidable joie de vivre, the flowers and olive trees in his garden, blooming female flesh, and the rosy cheeks of children.

After Cézanne, an entire swarm of early twentieth-century artists came to seek out the charged Provençal atmosphere and reinvigorate painting. Matisse, Dufy, Braque, Derain, Chagall, Picasso, and later Nicolas de Staël—all came here to work, together or in solitude, to remake the world, to confront their visions of it, even if there was sometimes disagreement over the results.

Matisse spent the summer of 1904 in the villa of La Hune, which Signac had bought in Saint-Tropez. He painted the bay, olive trees, and pines, but not in a pointillist idiom, which irritated Signac. It seems that Matisse was so upset by his reaction that during a walk he executed *Le Goûter,* one of his first studies for the very pointillist *Luxe, calme et volupté.* Signac, this time quite pleased, bought the canvas the following year.

In the spring of 1905 Albert Marquet, drawn above all by the bouillabaisse and the young women of the rue Pavé d'Amour, left Paris for Marseilles, then Saint-Tropez. "In these French tropics," he wrote, "we become tropical people." But it seems the weather took a bad turn, he started to complain, and Signac again became annoyed. "I can't really understand this correlation between art and the barometer," he wrote Matisse. "In my view it's futile and dangerous to fight against nature in this way." But the sun came out again and Marquet celebrated on July 14 by dancing the farandole with Signac and his wife.

Derain, who first went south to work with Matisse in Collioure, passed subsequent summers in L'Estaque, Cassis, and Martigues, where he discovered "a new conception of light that consists of the following: the negation of shadow." After attracting his friend Vlaminck to Martigues, he reproached him for seeing the South with northern eyes: "Your paintings of the Midi make it resemble Chatou."

Picasso reencountered his mythological obsessions in Antibes. "It's strange, in Paris I never draw fauns, centaurs, or mythological heroes. It's as though they thrived only here. Each time I arrive in Antibes, this antiquity reasserts its hold over me."

Braque painted olive trees, Derain cypresses and fishing boats, Matisse and Dufy windows opening onto the sea, while almost everyone painted L'Estaque. But then the specific subjects mattered little. After van Gogh, who had rightly thought the Midi could engender "the painting of the future, a colorist such as there's never been before," they all struggled with this dazzling light, which generates inner colors still more vibrant than reality. For some this quest would lead to increased wisdom and serenity, for others to an exacerbation of hallucinatory pain that banished all hope.

"Color is where our brain and the universe come together."—Cézanne

The first explorer of this pictorial Mediterranean was Signac. A passionate sailor, he came down the Midi canal on the *Olympia* in the spring of 1892 and discovered Saint-Tropez, "the eighth wonder of the world," which was then a small fishing port accessible only by sea. Even in Colette's day there was only a single road leading to it. "If you want to leave again you must go back the way you came. But will you want to?" When Françoise Sagan in her turn discovered the village, at the end of a chaotic main highway (Nationale 7), it was still a marvelous oasis where, from the terrace of the Escale—the only café—she could watch the old women knit and the fishermen unload their catch. "That was to be the last summer one saw people working," she wrote. Subsequently, Roger Vadim made *And God Created Woman* there and Brigitte Bardot bought La Madrague. Ever since, if one wants to love Saint-Tropez, one must go there in the spring, winter, or fall at dawn, or in one's dreams.

Bonnard also visited Signac there; although he was already familiar with Spain, Algeria, and Tunisia, it was as though he were seeing the Mediterranean for the first time: "I've had my taste of the Thousand and One Nights: the sea, the yellow walls, the reflections as full of color as the light." He returned there every year, finally settling for good in his pink and white house in Cannet, with its view of the sea and the jetty of the Esterel inlet, an ancient haunt of bandits guarded by the wicked fairy Esterelle, described by Frédéric Mistral as a "bitter enemy of man, haunting barren sites and crowning herself with nettles."

Looking through the agendas that Bonnard always carried about with him (they survive for the years 1925 to 1946), it is easy to imagine the general rhythms of his life but difficult to reconstitute its particulars, even vaguely. We are told of the daily weather (beautiful, cloudy, showers, mistral, rain) and what he needed to buy: wax, erasers, cheese, shirts, honey. A foggy Sunday inspired in him the following disabused observation: "The moment one declares oneself to be happy, one ceases to be so." On a Thursday in September he drew a goat with very horizontal ears and a rabbit with vertical ones, and often he inserted images of a woman, always the same one, his wife Marthe; we see her at a table with a cat, in a bathtub, cutting flowers. He maintained a prosaic correspondence with Matisse, discussing their respective colds and their difficulties obtaining provisions in wartime. And always, serious matters are evoked with such restraint that they almost disappear completely. All we learn about September 3, 1939, when France entered World War II, is that the weather was "rainy." And the Monday on which his dear Marthe died, he traced a small cross resembling a "plus" symbol and scribbled "beautiful" above it. He sometimes drew flowers and boats, and one day he noted: "When the weather's fine but cool, there is vermilion in orange shadows and violet in gray ones." He shared van Gogh's view that the strong light of the Midi obliged painters to "intensify their tones."

"I am conscious of expressing myself by means of light or rather in light, which seems to me like a block of crystal in which something is happening."
—— *Matisse*

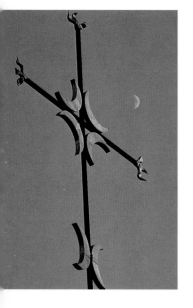

Matisse's Chapel of the Rosary Vence

When Bonnard wrote to him, Matisse was living in Nice, then in Vence, in a villa baptized Le Rêve—a pink house with green shutters surrounded by an unruly garden whose aviary would be immortalized by Cartier-Bresson. The interior, invaded by exuberant plants, bouquets of flowers, and fabric from the Pacific islands, was remarkably suggestive of a painting by Matisse. And this man of the North under a southern spell put into his painting everything the light of the Midi had to offer by way of voluptuous harmony. "I've always tried to give my works the lightness and gaiety of spring, so that one would never suspect the effort they cost me." Yes, the spring, which results from the obscure workings of sap right through the winter, and the charm of the *Seated Woman with Her Back to the Window,* the happy respiration of its sea—"That Matisse, he has very good lungs," said Picasso—they, too, were the result of sustained work.

Matisse, who didn't much care for churches, ended up designing one in its entirety—the Chapel of the Rosary in Vence—replete with ceramics, Virgin and child, and stained-glass windows of blue-yellow-green. And when he could no longer hold his brushes, he set to work in his room in Nice's Hotel Regina "sculpting" little pieces of colored cut paper into sensual forms, with results much admired by Nicolas de Staël: "Only two things are valuable in art: (1) the flash of authority, (2) the flash of hesitation. That covers everything. The one derives from the other, but at the summit the two can be distinguished quite easily. Matisse at age eighty-four manages to achieve this flash even with scraps of paper." In his rolling armchair, the floor around him strewn with bits of paper, he shaped women, flowers, birds, and waves with a large pair of scissors.

"The work goes by fits and starts, from slow terror to lightning flashes. It will take me years and years to get the clacking wind of your Provence."
—Nicolas de Staël to René Char, November 1953

It didn't take him years, he didn't have that much time. Settling in Antibes in September 1954, he committed suicide in March 1955, at age forty-one.

Like Bonnard, he had traveled extensively in sun-lit lands, but he, too, seems to have discovered *his* light for the first time in Provence, at Lavandou. During his first stay there he wrote to Jacques Dubourg, his dealer: "The light here is quite simply stunning. Color is literally devoured. As a result of one's retina being singed by the 'shattered blue,' as Char said, in the end one sees the sea as red and violet." He spoke again of this vision in a letter to René Char, with a hint of irony that was quickly swept away by the same exaltation: "All this brings to mind a postcard from a bazaar, but I want to remain imbued with this bazaar, this postcard, until the day I die. No kidding, René, it's unique, there's so much here. Afterward one is different." Having come a long way from the somber harmonies of his early work, he painted a scarlet sea at Martigues under an orange sky, and another orange sea under a black sky, and a red sea under a violet sky, and the perfect blue sky above the earth of Ménerbes, where in November 1953 he bought a fortified house on the prow of the village.

"I have difficulty getting the gulls just above the water."—Nicolas de Staël

From this point on things moved very quickly. In the spring of 1954, in time between trips and exhibitions, he did a great deal of drawing in Marseilles and Martigues. His son was born in April, but even so at summer's end he left Ménerbes for Antibes, where he rented a studio on the ramparts. From its terrace overlooking the Mediterranean he could see the stronghold called Fort-Carré, which he painted in nuances of nocturnal blue broken by flashes of white foam. In complete solitude he developed an increasingly fluid style, alternating violent colors with transparent grays of infinite subtlety. But above all, he struggled with "overbearing chance, like vertigo," which put him into "regrettable states of discouragement." It seems he was thinking about setting himself apart from the "abstraction gang," for he wrote Jacques Dubourg that he wanted to paint figures, men on horseback, and "markets full of people." In fact he painted gulls, the fort, magnificent boats, and still lifes—a hundred canvases in all.

On March 16, 1955, he wrote Jacques Dubourg once more, this time a very concise letter about a furniture maker near the ramparts from whom he'd ordered two chaises longues for Ménerbes, as well as problems with customs over some small chairs he'd purchased in Spain, also for Ménerbes. He offered a generalized thank-you, then slipped this in: "I don't have the strength to finish my paintings." That same day he threw himself from the height of his studio, leaving incomplete an immense canvas entitled *The Concert* with a piano, a string bass, and musical scores but no musicians—and not a trace of any "market full of people."

"We must live and create. Live to cry—as in front of this house with found tiles and blue shutters on a slope planted with cypresses."—Albert Camus

Staël and Camus had one great thing in common: the friendship of René Char. Camus had already run into this rugby player turned poet in the hallways of the publisher Gallimard, but it was only in 1947 on L'Isle-sur-la-Sorgue, not far from Ménerbes, that he got to know him and his disdain for the vanity and futility of Parisian life, a sentiment they shared.

Two years later, the doctor treating Camus's tuberculosis advised him to take the fresh air in Cabris, in the hills set somewhat back from the Mediterranean. There, in a house among olives and cypresses, Camus rediscovered something of his native Algeria: "In the afternoon the sun and light entering my room in waves, the veiled blue sky, the noise of children coming up from the village, the murmur of the fountain in the garden. And memories of Algiers come flooding back." Determined to heal himself, he adopted a draconian disciplinary regime and, between visits from Michel Gallimard, Jean-Paul Sartre, and Roger Martin du Gard, worked on *L'Homme révolté* (*The Rebel*), which promised to be "a curious little book."

But it was in Lourmarin, a town surrounded by vineyards at the foot of the Luberon hills, that he bought a house with his Nobel Prize money in 1958. Lourmarin was beloved of Jan Grenier, the Algiers philosophy professor who, after having equipped Camus to occupy a place in the front rank of the "big thinkers" of his day, became his friend—and a curious town it was, with one Catholic church, one Protestant church, and a single cemetery divided in two by a wall.

One side of the house seemed medieval, the other side indeterminate. It featured a terrace overlooking the valley of the Durance, the local château, and the cypresses of the cemetery. Camus had a sun carved above the door, parked his Citroën in the garage, and lodged in the stables a donkey that the actor Pierre Blanchar had sent him from Algeria.

*reflections
Martigues*

"There are no more straight lines, no more illuminated roads for beings departed from us. . . . The day prolonging the happiness between him and us is nowhere."
——*René Char,* L'Eternité à Lourmarin

In May of 1959 Camus settled in Lourmarin, once more imposing on himself a regime so monastic that he took to signing his letters "Frère Albert O.D." (Brother Albert of the Order of the Dominicans). Which didn't stop him from actively supporting the local soccer team and becoming friends with a blacksmith whose first name was worthy of Pagnol (César-Marius), as well as the gardener Franck Creac'h, an anarchist and autodidact from Brittany who had settled in Provence. Camus adopted this village, which suited him very well, as it did not Henri Bosco, another resident of Lourmarin who was much more distant. In August, after following the company performing *The Possessed* to Venice, then making the Parisian desert bearable by listening to flamenco singers with Michel Bouquet, he returned to Lourmarin to work on his adaptation of *Othello.* Back in Paris again, he wrote René Char about his increasing desire to leave the capital, which he found stifling.

He now contemplated dividing his time between Paris and Lourmarin, where in November he reverted to his monastic regime to facilitate work on a projected book, "Le Premier Homme," which he referred to as his "sentimental education" (alluding to Flaubert's novel of that name). On December 14, in Aix, he met with foreign students from thirty-eight different countries. He told them the creative process was a matter of much time and patience, of days and sometimes even months during which one wrote nothing, moving back and forth between the window and the writing table. This was to be his last public appearance, and shortly thereafter he gave his last interview to the American magazine *Venture.* With a strange prescience, when his wife Francine and her twins came to spend Christmas vacation with him, he confided to Francine that he would like to be buried in Lourmarin.

In Paris, when Emmanuel Berl expressed concern about "stories of roads" and cars, Camus reassured him by showing him his round-trip train ticket to Lourmarin and back. But he didn't use this ticket: on January 3, 1960, he headed for Paris in Michel Gallimard's Facel Vega. The next day the vehicle swerved inexplicably and crashed into two plane trees in succession. Farther down the road, in a leather briefcase covered with mud, were found a hundred and fifty manuscript pages of his incomplete book, "Le Premier Homme."

For the inhabitants of Lourmarin, burials tended to revive old tribal disputes. But the day Camus was buried, peace reigned. The anarchist Franck Creac'h carried the coffin alongside a Catholic he usually held in contempt, the whole soccer team was there, and the death knell rang out not from the Catholic or the Protestant church but from the clock tower dominating the village.

Today, Camus rests forever in the small cemetery whose cypresses he could see from his house, and his grave is overgrown with rosemary.

"Here in Redonne, I'm more alone and farther away from everything than I'd be in the depths of Brazil."—Blaise Cendrars

Alone, far from everything, and happy as never before. In 1927, between two voyages to Brazil, Cendrars moored in Redonne, the little fishing village he'd discovered in a cove close to Marseilles. He came to finish writing *Le Plan de l'aiguille (The Plane of the Needle),* but he ended up writing absolutely nothing. In fact, he gave himself over to game of *pétanque,* bouts of drinking pastis, and long walks in the wild with his dog Volga.

This great seafaring wanderer, who had traveled the four corners of the globe, from the Americas to China, from Siberia to the Sargasso Sea, also dropped anchor in Provence, in reality as well as in the realm of dreams. In *Carissima,* which he left unfinished, he narrated the exodus of the Magdalen, Martha, Lazarus, and all those fleeing Jerusalem, recounting how they crossed the Mediterranean, landed at the future Saintes-Maries-de-la-Mer, and dispersed to Marseilles, Tarascon, Arles, Aix, and Sainte-Baume.

In 1917, a decorated war hero with his right arm amputated, he was sent to convalesce in Cannes, which he soon left for the Villa Veranda, 26 avenue des Fleurs, Nice. It was here that he got his start in the movies, working with Abel Gance. And it was here that Modigliani, ill with tuberculosis, also came to recuperate. In July 1918 the two of them were often seen striding up and down the quay that dominates the port. Both wore striped sailor outfits, and Cendrars, his face lined, his arm cut off above the elbow, sported a turtle dove on his shoulder.

When he first returned from Brazil in 1925, he could be seen on the small, unfrequented beach at La Garoupe, where the American painter Gerald Murphy and his wife Sara threw extravagant parties in their Villa America. Here, with his friend Fernand Léger, he rejoined Picasso, Hemingway, Stravinsky, Dos Passos (his great admirer), and Fitzgerald, who took Murphy as the model for Dick Diver in *Tender Is the Night.*

After writing a few long articles for *Paris-Soir,* he planned to sail around the world on a three-masted schooner. All the preparations were made, the *Passat* was scheduled to cast off on September 7, 1939, but when the day arrived Cendrars was already a war correspondent in the Ardennes. He spent the rest of the war in Aix-en-Provence, writing nothing, in despair over the conditions of the armistice, hunted by the Germans, keeping track of military movements by means of maps tacked up on his kitchen wall—until the day in August 1944 when the Americans entered Aix and his fellow reporters joyously invaded his kitchen.

In October 1945 he received a letter of breathless admiration, expressed in a mixture of audacity and timidity, from an eighteen-year-old enlisted man named René Fallet. He said he had only "published two poems in a third-rate collaborative volume" but had "exalted poetic ideas." As soon as he was out of uniform, the young man rushed to Aix to see Cendrars. They went to a bistro, Fallet inserted a coin in a slot machine, and about a kilo more poured out. Favorably impressed, Cendrars resolutely extended his single hand (which he called "*ma main amie,*" "my friendly hand") and subsequently helped his admirer become the celebrated writer René Fallet, who would always call Cendrars "*patron.*"

And then a young unknown photographer arrived in Aix, Robert Doisneau. While waiting for Cendrars to return from a spree in Marseilles, Doisneau photographed the narrow streets of the old city and the sites associated with Cézanne, from the Jas-de-Bouffans to Mont-Sainte-Victoire. By pure chance, after three days he ran into Cendrars wrapped in barber's towels. He could finally offer him the bottle of rum he'd been carrying about since leaving Paris. Doisneau photographed Cendrars in front of his car, in his kitchen, at the market with his basket of provisions, without realizing that these photos would become known around the world. And then, enthusiastic about the suburban photographs of "this boy who has genius," Cendrars found him a publisher and wrote the text for his book *La Banlieue de Paris (The Suburbs of Paris).*

"Dear Henri Miller, people haven't kept up. They want me to be in the brush. They're fifty years too late. I'm at home. . ."—Blaise Cendrars

In 1947 there began, between Aix-en-Provence and Big Sur, between Cendrars and Miller, a correspondence that would continue uninterruptedly for twelve years. The next year Raymone—the woman of his life, whom Cendrars met in 1917 and married (in 1949, finally), and who would remain with him to the end of his life—settled in Villefranche-sur-Mer. And it was in Saint-Segond, above Villefranche, that Cendrars found his perfect spot: a roadway winding up through the bougainvilleas, a gate opening onto a kind of wild garden, the dog "Wagon-lit" playing with a tiny cat, and Raymone serving to his friends—Doisneau, Pierre Seghers, Malaparte, and many other journalists, travelers, and writers—the ritual beverage: white wine and sugared lemon juice. In *Le Lotissement du ciel (The Parceling of Heaven)*, Cendrars reminisced about the many-colored birds, the snakes, and the little she-ass Didine who brayed at his window every morning—his paradise on earth.

The House in the Vineyard

They're all gone now—the one-armed man in his striped shirt, the painters, the marquis, the man who spoke to the olive trees and the one who didn't want to save the little goat—and Provence is no longer what it was. Or so we're told. People say it's been invaded, disfigured, overcrowded, loved only too well. All this is doubtless true. But after all, no one compels us to visit Les Baux on a Sunday in August, in shorts, with a sack of provisions over our shoulder. "Invasions" can be effected with a certain discretion, and Provence the beautiful still exists—as seen in this book's pictures. It's all the blues of the sky and the ocher of the earth, sun and shadow dancing over a pink wall, a cypress that will never leave the tiny shack over which it keeps watch. It's this house in the vineyard where you, too, have come in search of light and paradise.

Speaking of which, it's four o'clock in the morning, dusty, and all is silence—the house, the road, the vineyard rolling in waves over the hills, and you dreaming in the semidarkness of your bedroom. But suddenly all hell breaks loose—preparations for battle. Your nerves tense, you try to make out what's happening. It reminds you, minus a few decibels, of the urban cocktail of rumbling trucks, cranes, and pneumatic drills. Here? In this wilderness? You open the shutters energetically and the memories flood back . . . The vineyard, of course . . . You've been spotted by the workers: a peasant gestures playfully to you from the top of his tractor. The fine fellow is obviously content. Even though it's four a.m. and the dust is rising, even though vacations are supposed to be restful, acknowledge him with good grace and smile. If it weren't for him, you'd have slept right through the last cicada and missed a superb spectacle: the phantom gray preceding the dawn, the torpid transparence bleeding into that marvelous light, that imperturbable blue of the Provençal sky.

FIELDS

pages 42-43
wheat fields
near Vaison-la-
Romaine

*farm
Le Barroux*

44

In general, geometry is an exact science. Here it indulges in dreams, heightened by chance and the providential juxtaposition of colors. The fourth side of the square isn't straight, it follows the road winding toward the house. The lines of brown furrows—brown laced with violet—mold themselves to the gentle incline of the hill. A solitary tree rises from the tawny ground with a stubborn air, as if determined to live out its existence just there, in the middle of nowhere. And when a field is allowed to go to seed, it's invaded by impressionist flowers that tremble in the sun: corn poppies from the Alpilles or Vauvenargues. But there are also cultivated flowers, which are picked on the hottest days of summer to make perfume, while a peasant, stationed between the shadow and the light, brings to mind a similar figure described by Giono: "He is standing in front of his fields. He wears full pants of brown corduroy and seems dressed in a fragment of his labors."

overleaf
farm
Mont Ventoux region

farm
Sault

farm
Mont Ventoux region

road in the
Camargue region

vineyards and fields
Les Baux-de-Provence   5 1

*poplars forming
windbreaks in a field
Sault*

tree-lined road
near Arles

poppies
Les Alpilles

olive grove and poppies
Les Alpilles

poppies
Vauvenargues

field of flowers
Lubéron region

*gathering flowers
near Saint-Rémy-de-
Provence*

farmer
near Saint-Rémy-de-
Provence

LAVENDER
AND
SUNFLOWERS

pages 60-61
lavender and sunflowers
Mont Ventoux region

sunflowers
Saint-Rémy-de-
Provence

62

Lavender has a delightful smell as well as many other fine qualities. There is male or spike lavender, whose oil was used as a dilutant by Renaissance painters. Some maintain it was this that imparted a particular brilliance to Rubens's colors. There's also a female or medicinal lavender, widely used in inhalants for the treatment of bronchitis and in skin liniments. It's even claimed that rubbing a bit of this lavender between one's fingers will provide relief for a dog bitten by a snake, but this seems doubtful. And then from June to September these violet clouds, these rotund masses become the province of working bees.

Oil is also fabricated from sunflowers, which obsessed van Gogh, who eventually managed to instill in Gauguin something of his fascination with them, while Colette wrote of them that their round centers seemed like "black honey cakes"—a rapturous, radiant flower multiplying the sun a thousandfold, following its path from dawn to dusk.

field of lavender
Valensole

lavender
Valensole

wheat and lavender
Mont Ventoux region

lavender
Vaucluse plateau

field of lavender
and wheat
Mont Ventoux region

field of lavender
Mont Ventoux region

70

lavender
Mont Ventoux region

lavender harvest
Mont Ventoux region

pages 74-75 (top)
sunflowers
Rhône River valley

page 75 (bottom)
sunflowers
Ménerbes

sunflowers
Saint-Rémy-de-
Provence

76

sunflowers
Les Alpilles

overleaf
sunflowers
Rhône River valley

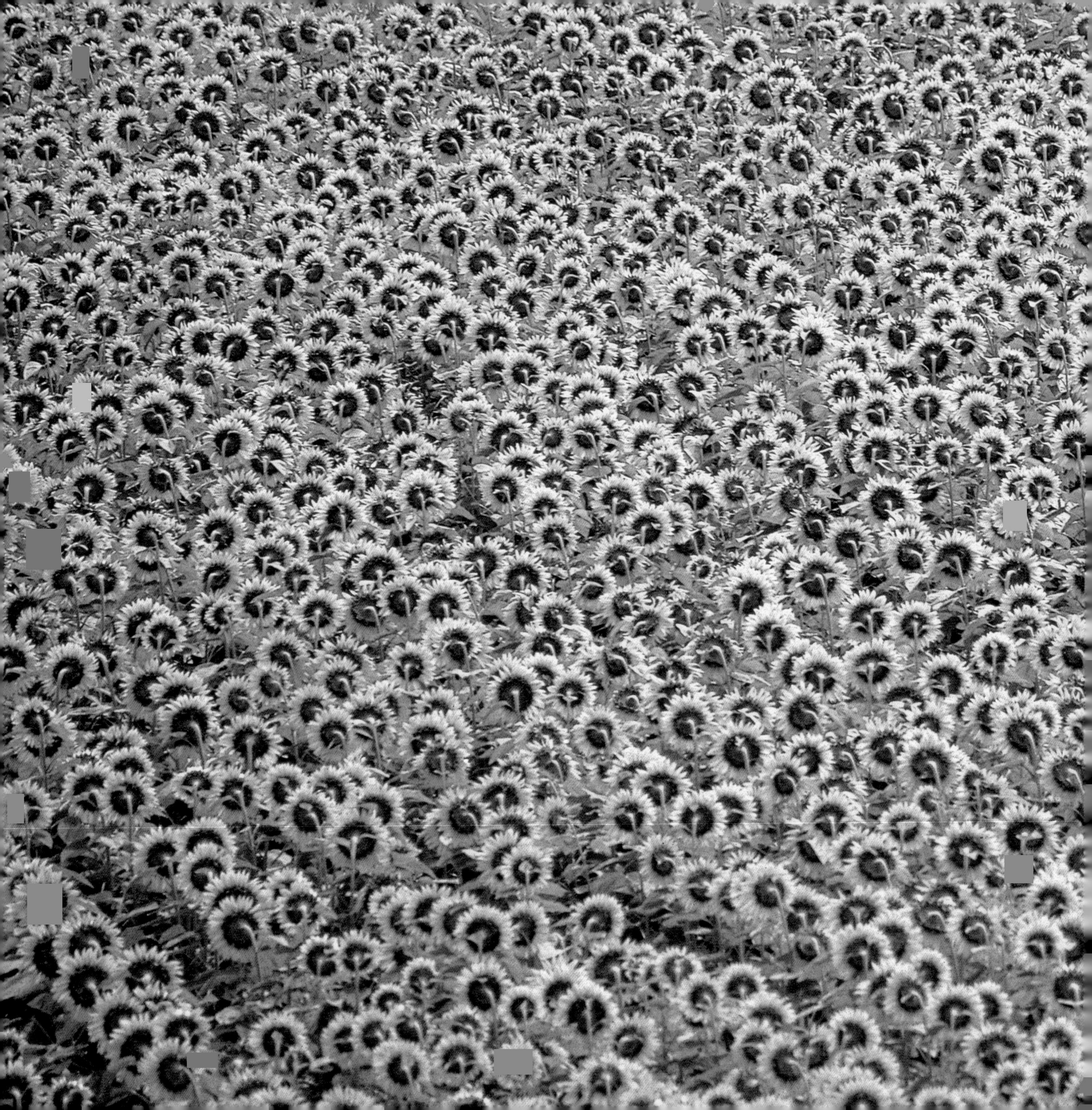

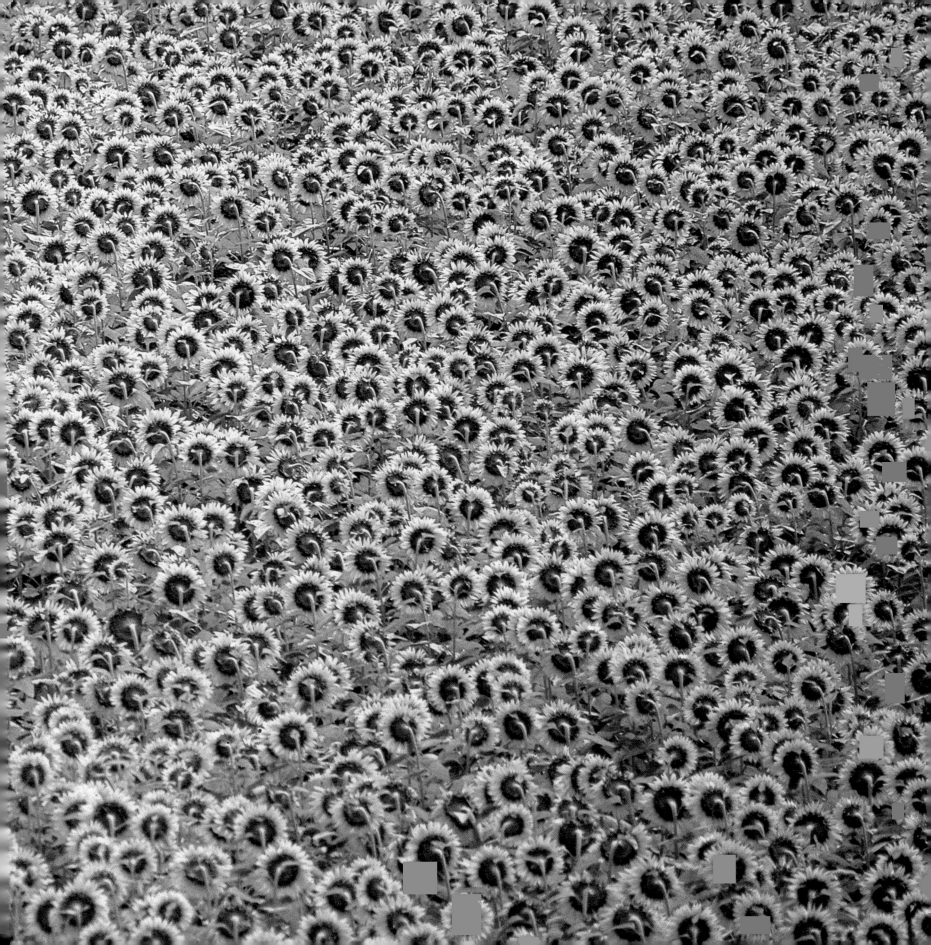

FARM LIFE

pages 80-81
sheepherder
Mont Ventoux

cow in barn
near Sault

shepherd arrives with his migrant flock, and a dog relaxing in the parched grass gazes imperiously at the photographer. Then the shepherd heads off, perhaps toward the stone house weathered by thirty-six thousand seasons at the foot of the Dentelles de Montmirail.

It's a bit surprising to find a cow and a goat here. They bring to mind imagery—the thick grass and animated skies of Normandy—that's at odds with the pure blue and the beating rays of the Midi. On the other hand, Provence could have been created expressly for cats. These animals know how to live, they love extreme heat. Could there be a happier earthly vision than that presented by chameleon-like tomcats (gold-brown against pinkish brown) blending into the sunlight and the curved roof tiles? When one thinks that there are regions where clouds prevail and the tiles are flat . . .

*goat and cow
near Sault*

*rooster
near Sault*

cats on farmhouse roof
near Sault

dog guarding barn
near Sault

overleaf
sheepherder
Mont Ventoux

WINDOWS

pages 88-89
windows and walls
Roussillon

window
Lourmarin

90

If windows are the soul of houses, then the soul of Provence is lavender blue, golden yellow, violet, and scarlet, sometimes decked out with flower boxes or adorned with cats, always opening onto mysteriously dark interiors. Sometimes a balcony traces a black filigree against the faded white of walls and shutters. In the asylum of Saint-Rémy, the windows do not have bars behind their pale blue swinging doors, but such was not the case for van Gogh's room: "Through the iron bars of the window I can take in an enclosed wheat field, a perspective suggestive of van Goyen, above which each morning I see the sun rise in all its glory." In Les Baux, a crumbling wall now allows azure rather than murderous invaders to pass through it. In Roussillon, a shutter that may never have been opened has unknowingly become, with the passing years, the bearer of a painter's dream: the perfection of a blue that has given way triumphantly to patches of red that are simultaneously brilliant and faded.

window
Roussillon

window
Roussillon

93

windows
Martigues

women chatting
Villefranche

window
Monieux

window
Saint-Etienne-du-Grès

window
Lourmarin

windows
Arles

windows
Tarascon

windows
Saint-Rémy-de-
Provence

window
Ménerbes

window
Les Baux-de-Provence

window
Roussillon

102

The Palace of the Popes
Avignon

window in Saint-Paul-
de-Mausole
monastery / convalescent
home, where
van Gogh lived
Saint-Rémy-de-
104   *Provence*

window
Les Baux-de-Provence

window
Les Baux-de-Provence

window
Riez

VILLAGES

pages 106-107
farmhouse near
Eygalières
Les Alpilles

village scene
Bonnieux

108

Sometimes everything blurs into monotony: the worn stone, the dust of the road rising in the heat, the pale ocher of the walls, the faded tiles—and an entire village beaten down by the sun, accepting this abuse with a resigned fatalism. And then in the market square everything comes alive and spruces itself up: cherries, raspberries, golden bread, peppers, and future ratatouilles (the perfume of their garlic and olive oil hovers in the air). The spices in baskets have as many colors as the bottled perfumes do scents. In front of the café on the square of Saint-Paul-de-Vence, Yves Montand has been captured playing *pétanque*—in a gesture like that of a sower, though slightly more exalted—and one longs for summer, one longs to take a seat on one of those wretched plastic chairs on the terrace, under the shadow of a tree, in the almost palpable torpor.

buildings
Gordes

rooftops
Eygalières   *111*

farmhouse near village
Sault

112

farmhouse near village
Sault

113

bell tower
Roussillon

114

street
Roussillon

parade on market day
Jouques

Yves Montand playing
the game of pétanque
Saint-Paul-de-Vence

village square
Biot

café
Roussillon

café
Uzès

café
Aurel

119

market day
Maussane-les-Alpilles

market day
Saint-Rémy-de-
Provence

121

fruit
Nîmes

olives
Saint-Rémy-de-
Provence

vegetables
Tarascon

herbes de Provence
Fontvieille

girl in traditional dress
Saint-Rémy-de-Provence

sheepherders'
celebration
Saint-Rémy-de-
Provence

perfume shop
Gourdon

perfume shop
Gourdon

STONEWORK

*pages 128-129
Roman Necropolis
at the Alyscamps
Arles*

*stone stairway
Gordes*

id van Gogh know when he painted the Alyscamps and the Trinquetaille bridge that he was following a legend-laden itinerary? In effect, the ancient inhabitants along the Rhône are said to have set coffins bearing their dead adrift in the river, along with a small sealed box containing money to compensate the people of Trinquetaille—a neighborhood in Arles—for fishing them out and giving them eternal rest in the Alyscamps. Saint Trophime, whose own legend was sculpted on the portal of the church dedicated to him in Arles, blessed a sepulcher there for Christians.

Sculpted angels and saints, faces both tormented and ecstatic, the Sisteron cliffs, the Gordes road climbing toward the sky, the magnificent decapitated bodies of Saint-Rémy, the gray tombs of the Alyscamps thrusting upward among the dead—the stones of Provence, whether Roman or Romanesque, whether worked by man or by centuries of exposure to the elements, are haunted by memory.

Roman relief and gargoyle
the Alyscamps
Arles

doorway,
Saint-Trophime
Arles

sculpted figure on
church façade
Saint-Gilles

doorway
Saint-Trophime
Arles

135

detail of Roman commemorative arch Saint-Rémy-de-Provence

136

mountain
Sisteron

overleaf
Roman amphitheater
Arles

137

*cypress trees flank a
stone chapel
Les Baux-de-Provence*

*ramparts of the Palace
of the Popes
Avignon*

141

Fenestrelle Tower
Uzès

Saint Sauveur cathedral
Aix-en-Provence

*Roman mausoleum
Saint-Rémy-de-
Provence*

*Roman commemorative
arch and mausoleum
Saint-Rémy-de-Provence*

143

*sarcophagi at
the Alyscamps
Arles*

*view of village
Saint-Paul-de-Vence*   145

cypress trees behind
a stone wall
Gordes

*Roman columns
at Glanum
near Saint-Rémy-de-
Provence*

147

CITIES

pages 148-149
bridge at dusk
Avignon

La Major Cathedral
Marseilles

Miraculously constructed by a child, destroyed by the furies of the Rhône and winter weather, the Avignon bridge is restored to us intact, thanks to a point of view that places the break and accompanying void outside the frame, thereby reviving the dream of an indestructible bridge of nineteen arches, while providing a persuasive visual rationale for Saint Bénezet's having been declared the patron saint of engineers and bridge builders.

At Avignon, in a Provence decimated by plague—it carried off Petrarch's Laura as well as the wife and two children of Nostradamus—and constantly crisscrossed by warring armies, the popes built themselves a palace, "the strongest, most beautiful house in the world," according to Froissart.

The church of Notre-Dame-de-la-Garde, a massive Byzantine-Romanesque pastiche designed by Espérandieu that wouldn't be out of place in a dream (or a nightmare), is encumbered by ex-votos left by the citizens of Marseilles in gratitude for countless maritime rescues and miraculous cures.

Memories of Cézanne hover over the fountains of Aix, while ghosts of van Gogh's companions in the Saint-Rémy asylum seem to inhabit its peaceful light—"honorable lunatics who always wear a hat, glasses, a cane, and a traveling outfit, rather as though they were at a seaside resort."

roses on tree trunk
Aix-en-Provence

road
near Arles   1 5 3

Saint-Trophime
Cloister
Arles

Saint Sauveur Cloister
Aix-en-Provence

155

Saint-Paul-de-Mausole
monastery
Saint-Rémy-de-
Provence

Domaine Sainte-Anne
Arles

157

fountain
Arles

fountain
Aix-en-Provence

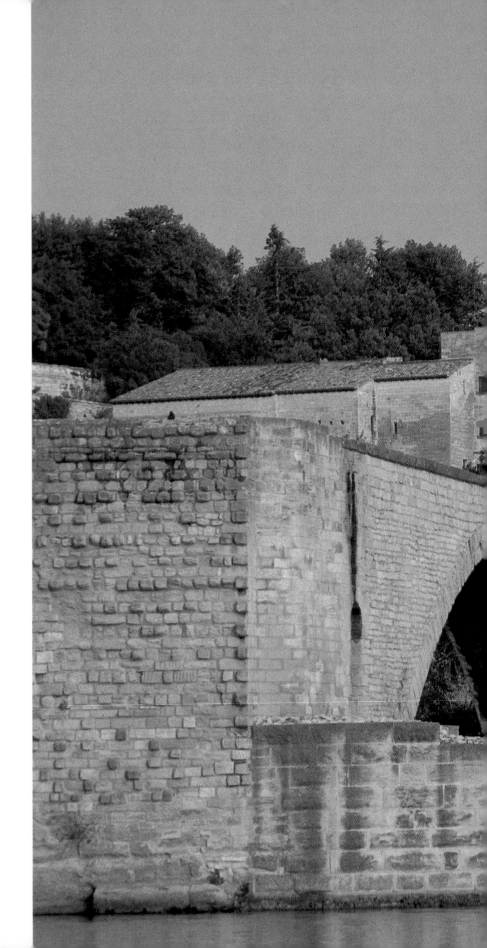

view of city
Avignon

LANDSCAPES AND SEASCAPES

pages 162-163
vineyard
Les Dentelles de
Montmirail

ocher cliffs
Roussillon

164

A ll the many Provences are here.

Cézanne's Mont Sainte-Victoire, which Giono saw as having "fantastic sails of white rock, like a phantom ship in full daylight." In front, a tree blends into this unreal environment with a Japanese grace.

White sails, real ones this time, tiny against the blue horizon, and a village perched among flowers—such were the two poles orienting Colette's happiness: "I love Provençal towns wedded to the dry summits of their hills. . . . But in summer I soon weary of seeing nothing but land; I begin to thirst for the sea, for its inflexible horizontal suture, blue against blue."

The blaze of ocher quarries, the rocky chaos of Baux-de-Provence, where Cocteau made *Le Testament d'Orphée (The Testament of Orpheus),* his last film. A house in a surrealist night suggestive of Magritte's *The Dominion of Light.* A white cloud delicately brushing against the Dentelles de Montmirail—such, at any rate, is the designation used on the side of Beaumes-de-Venise; on the other side they're known as the Dentelles de Gigondas.

And then there's that exceptionally clear light that bathes both earth and sky. Almost every spring, Bonnard painted the same almond tree flowering in his garden. Working on the last canvas in this series in the year of his death, he still sought to uncover the secret of the vibrating colors in this light: "That green, on the patch of ground in the lower left, doesn't work. It needs some yellow . . ."

Cross of Provence
Sainte-Victoire
mountains

ocher deposits
Roussillon

166

red earth
Sainte-Victoire
mountains

167

vineyards in early morning Les Dentelles de Montmirail

stairway on cliff
Les Baux-de-Provence

broom in bloom,
La Roque Alric
Beaumes-de-Venise

eroded cliffs
Les Baux-de-Provence

172

*cliffs along the
Mediterranean Sea
Cassis*

sailboats on the
Mediterranean Sea
Marseilles

sailboats in the old port
Marseilles   175

Roman mausoleum
at sunset
Saint-Rémy-de-
Provence

courtyard at night
Sault

PHOTOGRAPHERS'S NOTE

At first we came to Provence as a tribute to van Gogh, Matisse, Cézanne, and Picasso. We, too, were drawn to the region that drew so many before us—because of the light, the color, the joy; the sea and the land. A place where farmers are artists shaping their fields. Over the years, throughout the seasons, each return to Provence now feels like coming home. Yet each time there is the discovery of a new dimension. And always we try to capture the sense of the place—the essence of OUR Provence.....

Sonja and Angelo

ACKNOWLEDGMENTS

Our great thank you to Susan Costello for believing in this book and pulling it all together. We are also grateful to Patricia Fabricant for her talent and enormous patience and to Marike Gauthier for her good advice and generous contribution of time to the project. And we are indebted to Robert Abrams for allowing us to create our book.

We would like to say "thank you" to all our friends for their encouragement. We would also like to express our appreciation to our friends at the IMAGE Bank. And we send a special "thank you" to our French friends for their help: Danielle and Michel Droy; Anne-Sarah Fayet; Huguette and Alfred Giuliato; Andrée and Pierre Liardet; Jacques Lumia and his band—sapeurs - pompiers de Miramas; M. and Mme. Menant; Myriam and Patrick Thiant; and the many friendly "Provençaux".

INDEX

Page numbers in *italics* refer to illustrations

Aeschylus, 16
Aix-en-Provence, 31, 38, 39, 40, 151, *153, 155, 158-59;* Cézanne's studio in, *12;* Saint Sauveur cathedral in, *142, 155*
Alcazar café (Arles), 18
Allégret, Marc, 24
Les Alpilles, *4,* 16, *53, 54-55,* 77, *106-7*
Alyscamps (Arles), *9,* 18, 26, 131, *132, 134, 145;* Necropolis at, *128-29*
Amphitheater (Arles), *138-39*
And God Created Woman, 33
Angèle, 24
Antibes, 14, 22, 32, 35
Arbres (Prévert), 22
Aristotle, 16
Arles, 39, *53, 97, 152-53, 159;* Alyscamps in, *9,* 18, 26, *128-29,* 131, *132, 134, 145;* Daudet's windmill near, 26, *27,* 28; Domaine Saint-Anne in, *157;* Roman amphitheater in, *138-39;* Saint-Trophime in, 131, *132-33, 135, 154;* Trinquetaille neighborhood in, 131; van Gogh in, 15-16, 18-20; Van Gogh Square in, *10-11*
Arletty, 21
Aubagne, 14, 25
Aubignane, 24
Audiberti, Jacques, 22
Aurel, *119*
Avignon, 14, *160-61;* bridge at, 26, *148-49,* 151; Palace of the Popes in, *103, 141*

Banlieue de Paris, Le (The Suburbs of Paris) (Cendrars and Doisneau), 40
Bardot, Brigitte, 33
Barrault, Jean-Louis, 21
Barres-de-Saint-Esprit, 24
Le Barroux, *44*

Barthelasse, 26
Bastides Blanches, 22
Baux, counts of, 16, 17
Les Baux-de-Provence, 16-17, 26, 41, *50-51,* 91, *101, 104, 105, 140,* 165, *170, 172*
Beaumes-de-Venise, 165, *170-71*
Bénezet, Saint, 26, 151
Berl, Emmanuel, 38
Biot, *118*
Blanchar, Pierre, 36
Bonnard, Marthe, 33-34
Bonnard, Pierre, 33-34, 35, 165
Bonnieux, *1, 108*
Bosco, Henri, 38
Bouquet, Michel, 38
Braque, Georges, 22, 31, 32
Brasseur, Pierre, 21
Breton, André, 29

Cabris, 36
Cagnes-sur-Mer, 31
Camargue, 14, 26, *51*
Camus, Albert, 36-39; death and burial of, 38-39
Camus, Francine, 38
Cannes, 39
Cannet, 33
Carco, Francis, 15
Carissima (Cendrars), 39
Carné, Marcel, 21
Cartier-Bresson, Henri, 34
Cassis, 32, *173*
Cendrars, Blaise, 39-41
Cendrars, Raymone, 40
Cézanne, Paul, 31, 32, 33, 40, 151, 165; mistral and, 17, 18; studio of, *12*
Chagall, Marc, 22, 32
Chapel of the Rosary (Vence), *34*
Char, René, 35, 36, 38
Chateaubriand, François de, Vicomte, 24
Chateaurenard, *121*
Chopin, Frédéric, 24
cicadas, 13
Cocteau, Jean, 165

Colette, Sidonie-Gabrielle, 13, 14-15, 63, 165
Colline (Hill of Destiny) (Giono), 22
Collioure, 32
Concert, The (Staël), 36
La Coste, 29
La Crau, 16
Creac'h, Franck, 38-39
Cross of Provence, *166*
cypress trees, 20, *146*

Dante Alighieri, 16
Daudet, Alphonse, 18, 25-28; windmill of, 26, *27,* 28
Demosthenes, 22
Les Dentelles de Gigondas, 165
Les Dentelles de Montmirail, 83, *162-63,* 165, *168-69*
Derain, André, 32
Diurnes (Day Pieces) (Picasso and Prévert), 22
Doisneau, Robert, 40
Dominion of Light, The (Magritte), 165
Dos Passos, John, 39
Dubourg, Jacques, 35-36
Dubout, Albert, 24
Dufy, Raoul, 32
Duhamel, Marcel, 22
Dumas, Alexandre, 16
Durance, 23

Enfants du paradis, Les (Children of Paradise), 21
Escalier, Patience, 18
Espérandieu, 151
L'Estaque, 31, 32
Esterelle, 33
Eternité à Lourmarin, L' (Char), 38
Eygalières, *106-7, 110-11*

Fallet, René, 40
Fanny, 24
Farria, Abbé, 23
Femme du boulanger, La (The Baker's Wife), 24
Fenestrelle Tower (Uzès), *142*

"Feuilles mortes, Les" ("Autumn Leaves"), 22
Fitzgerald, F. Scott, 39
Flaubert, Gustave, 23, 24, 38
Fontvieille, *123*
Fort-Carré, 35
Fort Saint-Nicolas (Marseilles), 23
Froissart, Jean, 151

Gallimard, Michel, 36, 38
Gance, Abel, 39
Gard, Roger Martin du, 36
Gauguin, Paul, 17, 18-20, 63
Géraldy, Paul, 15
Giono, Jean, 14, 22-23, 24, 25, 45, 165
Glanum (near Saint-Rémy-de-Provence), *147*
Gordes, *5,* 111, *130,* 131, *146*
Gourdon, *126, 127*
Goûter, La (Matisse), 32
Grenier, Jan, 36
Grignan, 17
Grignan, Madame de, 17
Grimaldi, Château (Antibes), 22

Hemingway, Ernest, 39
Hercules, 16
Homme révolté, L' (The Rebel) (Camus), 36
Hotel Regina (Nice), 34
La Hune (Saint-Tropez), 32

If, Château d', 23
Inferno (Dante), 16
L'Isle-sur-la-Sorgue, 36

Jean le Bleu (Blue Boy), 24
Jofroy, 24
Jouques, *116-17*

Kosma, Joseph, 21

Lacoste, Château de, 28-29
La Fontaine, Jean de, 13
La Garoupe, 21, 39
Lamartine, Alphonse, 24

179

Lavandou, 35
lavender, *jacket, front, 2-3, 19, 60-61, 63, 64-73*
Léger, Fernand, 39
Lettres de mon moulin (Letters from My Mill) (Daudet), 25, 28
Lotissement du ciel, Le (The Parceling of Heaven) (Cendrars), 41
Louis XIII, king of France, 16
Loup River, 21
Lourmarin, 36-39, *90, 97*
Lubéron, *56-57*
Luxe, calme et volupté (Matisse), 32

La Madrague (Saint-Tropez), 33
Magritte, René, 165
La Major Cathedral (Marseilles), *150*
Malaparte, Curzio (Kurt Sackert), 40
Manosque, 22, 23
Mare au diable, La (The Devil's Pond) (Sand), 24
Marquet, Albert, 32
Marseilles, 23-24, 25, 32, 35, 39, 40, 151; La Major Cathedral in, *150;* port of, *174-75*
Martigues, 32, 35, *37, 94, jacket, back*
Matisse, Henri, 32, 33, 34; chapel designed by, *34*
Maussane-les-Alpilles, *120*
Mayo, 21
Mediterranean Sea, 14, 16, 17, 24, 33, 39, *173, 174-75*
Melville, Herman, 23
Memories of the North (van Gogh), 20
Ménerbes, 35, 36, *75, 100*
Michelet, Jules, 29
Miller, Henry, 40
Miró, Joan, 22
mistral, 17-18
Mistral, Frédéric, 33
Moby Dick (Melville), 23
Modigliani, Amadeo, 39
Monieux, 96
Montand, Yves, 22, 109, *116*
Monte Christo, Count of, 23
Mont Sainte-Victoire, 31, 165
Mont Ventoux, 13, 23, *30;* farm life in, *46-47, 49, 80-81, 86-87;* lavender and sunflowers in, *jacket, front, 2-3, 19, 60-61, 66-73*

Morières, 17, 18
Mouloudji, Marcel, 22
Murphy, Gerald, 39
Murphy, Sara, 39

Necropolis (Alyscamps, Arles), *128-29*
Nice, 21, 34, 39
Nîmes, *122*
Nostradamus, 151
Notre-Dame-de-la-Garde (Marseilles), 151
Nyons, 14

ocher, 29-31, *164, 165, 166*
olive trees, 14, 22, *54-55*

Pagnol, Joseph, 25
Pagnol, Marcel, 14, 24-25
Palace of the Popes (Avignon), *103, 141*
Paris-Soir, 39
pétanque, 23, 24, 39, 106, *116*
Petrarch, 14, 151
Picasso, Pablo, 22, 32, 34, 39
Pissarro, Camille, 31
Plan de l'aiguille, Le (The Plane of the Needle) (Cendrars), 39
Pont du Gard, 25
poppies, *53-56*
"Premier Homme, Le" (Camus), 38
Prévert, Jacques, 20-22, 23

Rais, Gilles de, 29
Raymond, 29-31
Redonne, 39
Regain (Harvest), 24, 25
Renoir, Auguste, 31-32
Le Rêve (Vence), 34
Revue aptésienne, 29
Rhone, 14, 17, 26, 131, 151
Rhone River valley, *74-75, 78-79*
Riez, *105*
Roman ruins, *9, 128-29, 132-39, 143, 147, 176. See also* Alyscamps
La Roque Alric (Beaumes-de-Venise), *170-71*
Roussillon, *88-89,* 91, *92, 93, 102, 114, 115, 118;* ocher deposits in, 29-31, *164, 166*

Sade, Donatien Alphonse François, Marquis de, 14, 28-29
Sagan, Françoise, 33
Sainte-Anne, Domaine (Arles), *157*
Sainte-Baume, 39
Saintes-Maries-de-la-Mer, 14, 17, 39
Saint-Etienne-du-Grès, 96
Sainte-Victoire mountains, *166, 167*
Saint-Gilles, *132, 135*
Saint-Loup, 25
Saint-Paul-de-Mausole monastery/convalescent home (Saint-Rémy-de-Provence), *6-7, 104, 156*
Saint-Paul-de-Vence, 20, 22, 109, 116, *144-45*
Saint-Rémy-de-Provence, *9, 58, 59, 62, 76, 99, 122, 124-25,* 131; asylum in, 20, 91, 151; Roman ruins in, *136, 143, 176;* Saint-Paul-de-Mausole monastery/convalescent home in, *6-7, 104, 156*
Saint Sauveur cathedral (Aix-en-Provence), *142;* cloister of, *155*
Saint-Segond (Villefranche), 40
Saint-Tropez, 14-15, 16, 32, 33-34
Saint-Trophime (Arles), 131, *132-33, 135;* cloister of, *154*
Sand, George (Amandine-Aurore-Lucile Dudevant), 24
Sartre, Jean-Paul, 36
Sault, *52, 112, 113, 177;* farm life in, *48, 82, 84, 85*
Seated Woman with Her Back to the Window (Matisse), 34
Seghers, Pierre, 40
Segonzac, Dunoyer de, 15
Seguin, M., 28
Série Noir, 22
Sévigné, Madame de, 17, 24
Signac, Paul, 16, 32, 33
Signoret, Simone, 22
Sirmonde, 29-31
Sisteron, *137*
Staël, Nicolas de, 14, 16, 32, 34, 35-36; suicide of, 35, 36
Stravinsky, Igor, 39
sunflowers, *jacket, front, 1,* 18, *19,* 20, *60-61, 62, 74-79*

Tarascon, 39, *98, 123*
Tartarin sur les Alpes (Daudet), 18
Tender Is the Night (Fitzgerald), 39
Testament d'Orphée, Le (The Testament of Orpheus), 165
Tourist Guide to Mount Ventoux, 13
Tourrettes-sur-Loup, 20-21
Trauner, Alexander, 21
Treille Muscate (Saint Tropez), 15
Trinquetaille (Arles), 131
Trophime, Saint, 131

Un de Beaumugnes (One from Beaumugnes) (Giono), 24
Uzès, *119;* Fenestrelle Tower in, *142*

Vadim, Roger, 33
Vaison-la-Romaine, *42-43*
Valensole, *64-65,* 67
Valley of Hell, 16
van Gogh, Theo, 15-16, 18, 20
van Gogh, Vincent, 13, 14, 15-16, 32, 34, 63, 131; at asylum of Saint-Rémy, 20, 91, 151; ear severed by, 18; Gauguin and, 18-20; mistral and, 17, 18; at Saint-Paul-de-Mausole monastery/convalescent home, *6-7, 104*
Van Gogh Square (Arles), *10-11*
Vaucluse, 21, 69
Vauvenargues, *56*
Vence, 22, 34; chapel designed by Matisse in, *34*
Venture, 38
Villa America (Garoupe), 39
Villa Veranda (Nice), 39
Villefranche-sur-Mer, 40, *95*
Vincennes, 29
vineyards, *50-51, 162-63, 168-69*
Visiteurs du soir, Les (The Evening Visitors), 21
Vivarais, 17
Vlaminck, Maurice de, 32

World War II, 20-21, 23, 33, 40

Zeus, 16
Zola, Emile, 23, 31

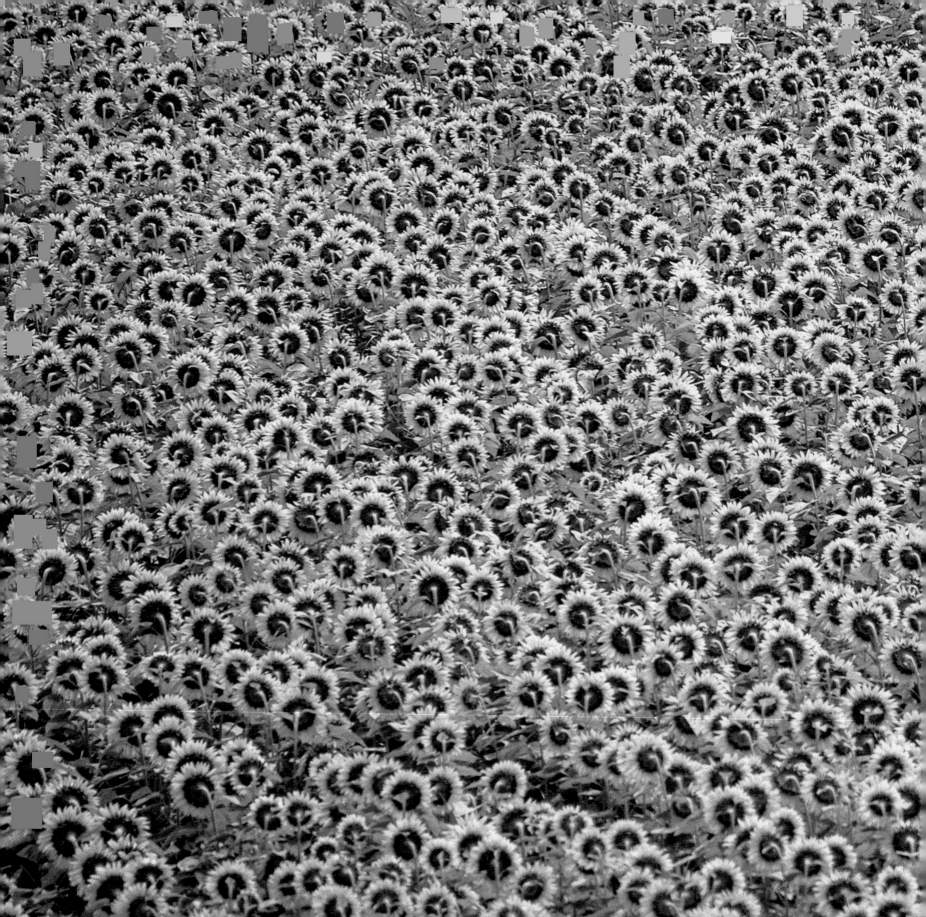